Stalybridge Band, from near Manchester, circa 1904. The band is said to have been the first all-brass band in the British Isles.

VILLAGE AND TOWN BANDS

Christopher Weir

Shire Publications Ltd

CONTENTS

Set in 10 on 9 point Times and printed in Great Britain by C. I. Thomas & Sons (Haverfordwest) Ltd, Press Buildings, Merlins Bridge, Haverfordwest.

ACKNOWLEDGEMENTS
The cover photograph is reproduced by kind permission of the Victoria and Albert Museum. Other photographs are acknowledged as follows: Crail Preservation Society, page 6; Local Studies Library of Nottinghamshire County Library, pages 7, 17; City of Manchester Local History Library, pages 8, 9 (top); Mr A. Henstock, pages 9 (bottom), 19; Tameside Local History Library, pages 1, 11, 30; Victoria and Albert Museum, page 12; Dorset County Library, page 15 (top); Grosvenor Museum, Chester, page 20; Gwynedd Archives Service, page 25 (top); British Library, page 32; Nottinghamshire Records Office (from Nottingham City Archives), page 3; Nottinghamshire Records Office (from Walkeringham parish records), page 13. The author also wishes to acknowledge the help of Andrew Leeming for many of the photographs in this volume, Brian Craven for the photographs on pages 1, 11 and 21, and Julian Marsh for the line drawing on page 24. Thanks are also due to Lorna Weir for typing the manuscript.

COVER: *Detail from 'The Village Choir', a painting by Thomas Webster RA, in the Victoria and Albert Museum, London. See also page 12.*

LEFT: *Jack Metcalfe (1717-1810), better known as Blind Jack of Knaresborough, was blind from the age of six as a result of smallpox. Yet he nevertheless taught himself to play the fiddle and supported his wife and family by performing at inns and fairs throughout Yorkshire. Even more surprisingly he turned to roadmaking in his later years and became famous for establishing a system of turnpike roads in the North of England.*

A voucher signed by the Mayor of Nottingham for a payment to be made to the town waits. Nottingham waits existed from at least 1501, when the three players were paid 6s 8d each. They played at mayor-making ceremonies, civic banquets and processions. Transcript: 'July 27th 1731. Mr Chamberlin Pay to Drumers 15 Shillings and the Trumpeters ten Shillings for the Day of Thansgivin for Drumin & Trumpitin yt Day and it shall be alowed in your Accts of Me William Barke Major.'

EARLY DAYS

The origins of band music are uncertain. The earliest bands may have drawn inspiration from town waits, some of which were founded in medieval times to provide music on ceremonial occasions. Norwich waits dated from at least 1408; at first there were only three musicians but by 1589 there were five players, and in that year they were commissioned to accompany Sir Francis Drake to Cadiz. By 1622 there were no less than sixteen players, their instruments comprising: four sackbuts, four oboes, two tenor cornets, one tenor recorder, two counter-tenor recorders and 'an old howboye (hautboy) broken', together with five chains and five flags — the chains being badges of office while the flags were used to decorate the instruments.

Most waits received only nominal wages: at Canterbury in 1498 the waits were paid just £1 each year. To supplement their income players performed at private engagements and may even have formed their own musical troupes or bands. But players in waits were usually bound by the restrictive practices of musicians' guilds, which tended to limit the influence of waits to within their own town boundaries. At Leicester waits were only allowed to play outside the town under a special licence, which was rarely granted, and no strangers were allowed to play inside the town. Waits continued until 1835, when they were abolished by the Municipal Reform Act. Ironically this piece of legislation benefited band music as players tended to form bands of their own from old waits, as for instance in York where Daniel Hardman formed a band of his own when the town waits were disbanded in 1833.

The eventual spread of band music is more likely to have been associated with the appearance of musicians attached to army regiments. Charles II is known to have heard army bands in France during his stay there in exile and is thought to have introduced them to England following his Restoration; certainly by 1678 a band of sorts was attached to the Horse Grenadiers, and other regiments soon followed suit. The sight of a military band playing while on the march was calculated to catch the attention of onlookers and may well have prompted any watching amateur musicians to form bands of their own. Although the evolution of military bands took an entirely different course to

Medieval musician, playing a pipe and tabor. The figure is inset into a leaded pane of the Betley-Tollet church window, Staffordshire, which depicts May Day revellers of old England.

domestic bands their influence was considerable in the early days.

The development of bands owes a great deal to the tradition of itinerant musicianship established as early as medieval times when minstrels wandered the land entertaining at fairs, tournaments, weddings and other functions. Medieval life left little time for people to do much more than just work and sleep so that entertainment came to be provided by strolling players, minstrels, jugglers and acrobats.

Eighteenth-century itinerant musician.

Itinerants played an important role in traditional culture, supplying news as well as entertaining and, in the case of musicians, spreading a knowledge of songs, tunes and musical expertise without which the evolution of bands would have been impossible. In some parish churches the musicians' skills were celebrated in windows and altar pieces, with portions illustrating both minstrels and their various musical instruments.

Popular amongst itinerant musicians were the pipes, the Scots favouring bagpipes while the Irish preferred their own traditional pipes, including the fearsome Great War Pipes or *piob mor*. Wales and Ireland both had an ancient heritage of harp music, producing many famous harpers. Cormac MacDermot, an Irish harper, won fame by being summoned to play at the court of Queen Elizabeth I and some years later he became court musician to James I. Such examples were however rare, especially in Ireland, where local courts subjected itinerants to astonishing cruelties. In 1656 Cornelius O'Brian, an Irish piper, was sentenced to twenty lashes and transportation to the West Indies, a journey from which few returned.

In England courts were less harsh, though the introduction of the Elizabethan Poor Laws did severely restrict the movements of itinerant musicians. These laws enabled parish officials to remove anyone from their parish who did not have a legal settlement and who seemed likely to become a burden on the poor rates. As a consequence itinerant musicians often fell victim to over-zealous parish overseers who had little concern for distinguishing genuine musicians from vagrants and landless beggars. Despite these difficulties countless itinerants continued to make a precarious living, playing their music wherever an audience could be found. Happily subsequent laws proved more enlightened and, although itinerants never regained the prestige of former days, the tradition of itinerant musicianship survived.

The town crier of Crail, east Fife, Scotland. This local character was once a familiar sight in the town's streets, combining both vocal and musical talents. His drum is preserved in Crail Museum.

This photograph, taken in the market place, Sutton, Nottinghamshire, shows the combined Scott and Limbs and Denman's Head Bands about 1864. At that time the town had no less than six bands.

COUNTRY BANDS

The first bands were composed largely of reed, wind and string instruments, though during the seventeenth century the use of brass instruments became common all over Britain, a development that gave rise to dismay in some quarters. The wit and antiquarian John Aubrey wrote: 'In Herefordshire and parts of the Marches; the Tabor and pipe were exceeding common. Many beggars begd with it: and the Peasants danced to it in the Churchyard on Holy-day-eves. Now it is almost lost: the Drumme and trumpet have putt that peaceable Musique to silence.' But not everyone shared Aubrey's opinion of the new music, for by the eighteenth century bands had become a lively and important part of village life in many counties. Composed of enthusiastic self-taught countrymen, they played at church services, fairs, dances, weddings, or wherever people gathered to pass the time of day.

While village bands were often only small family affairs, some quite large bands, with perhaps ten or more players,

grew up in local inns, where band practice was frequently encouraged by landlords eager to promote the quaffing of ale. One of today's best known bands, Besses o' th' Barn, began life in this way. Besses first appeared as Cleggs' Reed Band in the 1790s. Originally it was composed of three brothers, John, James and Joseph Clegg, with a few friends from the village of Besses o' th' Barn near Bury. Band practice was held in the local inn, also known as Besses o' th' Barn and from which the band is said to have taken its name when it changed to being an all-brass band in the nineteenth century. The village of Besses o' th' Barn has since been overtaken by the Manchester conurbation, although the band itself is now one of the leading brass bands in Britain, with a countless number of prizes and trophies to its credit. It is also one of the oldest bands still in existence.

For the most part, village bandsmen used traditional orchestral instruments, though the expense of buying new instruments was an ever present problem for

ABOVE: *The Besses o' th' Barn Band, 1860.*
OPPOSITE TOP: *Besses o' the' Barn Inn, where Besses Band is said to have practised and from which it may have taken its name.*
OPPOSITE BOTTOM: *A volunteer band marching through Ashbourne, Derbyshire.*

bandsmen. Richer players sometimes did buy their own instruments, but many bands purchased them by subscription, usually through a committee, which then loaned them to players. If a player contributed any of his own money towards the purchase of an instrument, his share was paid back to him when he returned it to the committee. This system was adopted by a Devon band formed in the village of Modbury in July 1838. Before the band's formation, committee members requested a quotation for instruments from Thomas Stockham, a West Country instrument maker. The most expensive instrument quoted for was a serpent, at £5 10s. A trombone was quoted at £3 5s, a French horn at £3, a bass horn at £2 2s and a clarinet at £1 15s. Stockham also guaranteed that 'the whole sum shall be perfectly packed in cases with Scales and Music.' To a farm labourer such prices would have seemed very high. The Modbury villagers, however, were not deterred and purchased an unusually large number of instruments: a serpent, a bass horn, two octave flutes, a trumpet, five clarinets, trombone, French horn, key bugle and a drum. Money was raised by subscription in

order to buy the instruments. Meetings of subscribers were held twice a year, on Christmas Eve and Midsummer's Eve, with subscribers being entitled to vote on all matters concerning the running of the band — on the basis of one vote for every five shillings subscribed; a limit of four votes per meeting was imposed. Modbury band was fortunate in that it had a healthy number of subscribers; lesser bands had to survive on a day-to-day basis.

Brass instruments were used by early village bands but they were of variable quality; and all were hampered by their lack of valves. In his poem 'The Village Fair' James Hurdis (1763-1801) writes of the 'groaning horn and twanking trumpet', suggesting the tone of these instruments was not all it might have been. But such criticisms are unlikely to have made much impression on either the bandsmen or their audiences. The intention, more often than not, was to attract a crowd, accompany a procession or provide accompaniment to dances; simple jigs, reels, marches or hymns were the musical fare of most village bands. Tunes were often played by ear or from manuscript books laboriously

Bell's Band, Bradley, Derbyshire. The dashing military-style uniforms illustrate the influence of military bands of the day.

copied out by the players themselves — the sacred and secular side by side. Performances must have been a tiring business, sometimes with a long tramp out to a neighbouring hamlet, performing for hours at a time, and often not returning home until dawn. For their labours bandsmen received little reward; a few pence for a performance was as much as most could expect. Payment came from various sources: local farmers, householders, sometimes the lord of the manor. However, for most bandsmen the opportunity to play a treasured instrument in front of an audience was probably reward enough. An additional attraction of playing in some bands was the chance to wear a uniform, which may have been anything from 'Sunday best' to a dazzling military style copied from one of the military bands of the day.

In the nineteenth and early twentieth centuries country bands were in demand for all kinds of occasions, even jubilee and coronation celebrations. In 1911 the Bainbridge Band of North Yorkshire was requested to play for the coronation celebrations at Middleham Castle. The band played all afternoon and then for a dance in the evening; returning by the 6 a.m. train to Bainbridge, the band was immediately back in action, leading a march through the village and playing for the rest of the day in the local celebrations. In some parts of Britain, especially the North of England, industrialisation led to the foundation of larger and more accomplished bands. Yorkshire's Black Dyke Mills Band began life in the village of Queensbury as Peter Wharton's Brass and Reed Band but rapidly rose to fame after the firm of John Foster's equipped it with new instruments and uniforms and renamed it after the mills. Unfortunately rural depopulation left some bands with only a handful of players, and some of these were often less able members. For country bands, change and progress brought with them uncertain futures.

A bizarre one-man band playing somewhere in south-east Lancashire about 1880.

Thomas Webster's painting 'The Village Choir', showing singers and musicians in the west gallery of Bow Brickhill church in Buckinghamshire.

CHURCH BANDS

Musicians had played in churches from medieval times but it was only in the sixteenth century that churches began to engage bands to accompany services. Their appearance became more common following an order issued by Queen Elizabeth I in 1561 which allowed the 'using or transposing of the rood-lofts'. The order made it possible for churches to imitate the great Tudor houses like Hardwick Hall which had ornate galleries from which minstrels or bands could entertain. While some of the resulting church galleries were quite grand, others were inevitably makeshift. In Edwalton, Nottinghamshire, the church band played in a converted loft set in a precarious position high above the front tower arch; and in it were huddled bassoonists, flautists, trumpeters and fiddlers. The music produced by such an ill assorted company can only be left to the imagination, though the ubiquity of church bands is evidence of their popularity.

One of the greatest champions of church bands was the novelist Thomas Hardy, whose family had participated in church band music since 1801, when his grandfather moved to Stinsford, near Dorchester, and found the state of church music to be in a deplorable condition; it consisted of an old man with an oboe playing in the gallery. Hardy's grandfather set about reviving Stinsford's church band, himself playing the bass-viol. He was later joined by his two sons, one of whom was the novelist's father. Hardy was too young ever to have heard the Stinsford band play but he did absorb his family's musical tradition; he learned to play the violin and often played at country dances in the company of his father and uncle. Hardy's experiences were written into one of his best loved novels, *Under the Greenwood Tree,* which portrays the lives of the Mellstock choir members and its old-established west gallery musicians. Mellstock, although a fictitious village, could have been any one of countless villages in Hardy's native West Country in the early nineteenth century. At Winterbourne Abbas, six miles from Dorchester, three performers played in the church gallery; these were J. Dunford, a thatcher (clarinet), W. Dunford, a shepherd (bass), and R. Tompkins, a farm labourer (flute). A neighbouring village, Winterbourne Steepleton, also supported a church band of some five or six members which continued to play until 1881. The two bands came under the supervision of the rector, who paid performers five shillings a year for renewing strings and reeds. Also near Dorchester, at Martinstown, church band boasted a company of twenty singers, four clarinets, a hautboy and a bass-viol; two clarinets played the air, two clarinets the counter-tenor and the hautboy played the tenor — an octave above the voice.

Bands playing at church functions were usually paid by the churchwardens and reference to this can be found in contemporary churchwardens' accounts and parish registers. Sometimes payment was made in kind. In the Nottinghamshire village of East Retford bandsmen playing in the parish church could look forward to a mug of hot toddy during the winter, though this tradition came to an abrupt end when on one occasion it resulted in the entire band breaking into a brisk polka in-

A page from a parish register for Walkeringham, Nottinghamshire, with a memorandum signed by the churchwardens and clerk as to the purchase of a bassoon and 'clarranett' for the parish singers, 3rd January 1809.

13

stead of the expected hymn.

But to Victorian churchgoers band music was thought little better than an 'unholy row' and by the second half of the nineteenth century church bands were fast disappearing; the organ and choir were considered a more dignified accompaniment to the serious business of religion. As a consequence churches all over the country had their galleries dismantled or simply allowed them to rot away; it was the end of an era of church music. The novelist Samuel Butler, who like Hardy was an ardent church band lover, noted the loss of galleries and their bands in *The Way of All Flesh*. When Theobald, the novel's principal character, becomes rector at Battersby in 1834, the church gallery was occupied by a choir and musicians; but by the end of Theobald's time there they have been replaced by a harmonium. The novel's narrator writes: 'Gone now are the clarinet, the violincello, and the trombone, wild minstrelsy as of the doleful creatures of Ezekiel, discordant but infinitely pathetic. Gone is that scarebabe Stentor, that bellowing bull of Bashan, the village blacksmith, gone is the melodious carpenter, gone the brawny shepherd with the red hair who roared more lustily than all . . . '

In towns some evangelical churches adopted bands but the country gentry were sensitive to changing fashion and the taste of upper-class Victorian society was for orchestras and ballrooms rather than band music. Church bands were particularly hard hit under these circumstances and were increasingly replaced by organs, even barrel organs in some places. Frequently the gentry contributed funds towards the installation of organs in their parish churches, a trend that reflected changing musical fashion. Faced with these difficulties church bands found it more and more difficult to survive and by the turn of the century they had become more of a curiosity than an integral part of village life.

View of Llanbister church, Powys, Wales, showing the west gallery.

RIGHT: *Thomas Hardy, the novelist, who was also a great church band enthusiast.*

BELOW: *St Paul's Church Band, Stratford, London.*

Consett Salvation Army Band, from County Durham, thought to be the first ever Salvation band. Note the helical or 'wrap-around' bass, which was popular for a short time in the late nineteenth century.

THE MUSIC OF SALVATION

An uneasy relationship between all types of music and the sabbath had existed right from Oliver Cromwell's time. In 1677 Charles II approved an Act of Parliament 'for the better Observation of the Lord's Day'; and thereafter it became usual for newly crowned monarchs to issue a proclamation 'for the Encouragement of Piety and Virtue and for the preventing and punishing of Vice, Profaneness and Immorality', to be read at church services and before the commencement of quarter sessions. Music was placed in an ambiguous position, with players facing fines and possibly imprisonment if they broke the sabbath peace. For band music, matters came to a head following performances, for the first time, in 1856 of brass bands in London's parks and recreation grounds. Other municipal authorities soon took up the idea and, as Sunday was for most people their only free day in the week either to play in a band or to listen to one, there was an immediate conflict with organisations like the Lord's Day Observance Society, headed by the Earl of Shaftesbury, and the Working Men's Lord's Day of Rest Association. Public

debates over the issue were stormy; meetings frequently broke up in violence and Shaftesbury's house was the subject of a virtual siege by his opponents. Supporters of recreation on Sundays formed the National Sunday League; cheap railway excursions were organised, musical concerts were staged and a campaign for the Sunday opening of museums and art galleries was launched. The row was bitter, dragging on for over half a century, and although band music continued to be played on Sundays it was never considered quite respectable by Victorian and Edwardian upper-class society.

Nonconformist reactions to Sunday music varied; with only the best of intentions many Methodist and Baptist musicians had joined temperance bands, yet were sometimes severely criticised for encouraging profaneness by playing on Sundays. Mr J. Rogers, bandmaster of Northampton Silver Temperance Band, offered encouragement to fellows in this predicament when he wrote to *Brass Band News* in November 1887. In his letter Mr Rogers admitted to grave misgivings when justices granted his band permission to give

William Booth (1856-1929), the founder of the Salvation Army, was a lifelong lover of bands and he often included them at his meetings.

Nottingham Memorial Halls Band, 1900.

a Sunday concert in Northampton Corn Exchange but confessed that all doubts were brushed aside after the concert's outstanding success. Behaviour at the concert was exemplary and surely better this, Mr Rogers maintained, 'than youngsters wandering the streets'.

Similar views were expressed by William Booth, the founder of the Salvation Army. Booth, a great lover of band music, called it 'the music of Salvation'; he recognised its potential in drawing crowds to his open-air meetings, and by the time he died, in 1912, Salvation Army bands had become a familiar sight all over the world. At Booth's funeral in London forty bands paid a last musical tribute to their lifelong patron.

Controversy, especially in the early days, was never far from Salvation Army bands. When a small group of evangelists began a series of unconventional open-air meetings in Salisbury during the spring of 1878 the citizens became alarmed; and their concern grew when the group introduced revivalist hymns to their programmes. Then, towards the end of the year, the Salvationists were joined by a formidable brass band composed of Charles Fry, by trade a master builder, and his

three sons. They were all devout Methodists but were nevertheless sympathetic to the Salvationists. The family had at one time split up, although some time before forming the band they had reunited in an attempt to revive the fortunes of their building business. Charles Fry himself was a more than capable musician, having played cornet in the First Wiltshire Volunteer Rifle Corps and having later been the leader of Alderbury village choir, near Salisbury. Whatever happened to the Frys' business, their band proved an unqualified success; by 1880 it had led to the creation of 'Salisbury Brass Band' and it was this band that followed Booth's progress in South Wales, in that same year, and which attracted crowds sometimes thousands strong.

The Salvation Army band movement spread with astonishing speed and by 1900 Army bands had become a familiar sight in most towns and cities.

In contrast to the resounding success of Salvation Army band music, chapel and temperance bands suffered a drastic decline. In the course of the nineteenth century chapels tended to drop their bands in favour of choirs, whilst temperance bands fell in number as the temperance movement lost its appeal. Some temperance bands had never taken themselves very seriously, and some experienced lapses, as Dr Spark, a contest adjudicator, discovered at Skipton in July 1888. In a report to the *Leeds Times*, Dr Spark complained that on his return train journey from Skipton to Leeds he had been set upon by thirteen 'thoroughly intoxicated' members of a temperance band, who had then continued to tear him apart 'limb from limb'. The band's members apparently objected to their low placing in the contest.

A few temperance bands did, however, survive the general decline of temperance music, notably Wingates Temperance Band. Wingates originated in Westhoughton, now in Greater Manchester, in 1873 when bible class members met to discuss a challenge to form a band and compete against a local secular band. The challenge was duly accepted, and, whatever the result of that competition, Wingates marched from strength to strength, establishing a national reputation as early as 1900 by winning third prize at the National Brass Band contest at Crystal Palace.

Ashbourne Salvation Army Band, from Derbyshire, 1884.

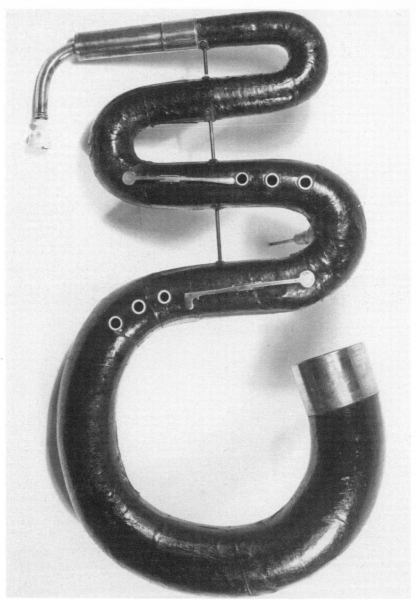

The serpent was a strange-looking musical instrument, much favoured by village and town bands. This particular serpent was used to accompany the village choir at Standlake in Oxfordshire.

A handsome cornet, still in use by a member of the Droylsden Band, from near Manchester.

MUSICAL INSTRUMENTS

Before the days of modern brass instruments bandsmen used whatever came to hand. Instruments had to be begged, borrowed or invented. Some of the more bizarre musical contraptions used in the early days have been handed down through successive generations and are now museum pieces. Strangest of all was the serpent, so called because of its serpent-like shape. It was made of wooden sections bound together by leather or joined by staples and glue with a mouthpiece of horn or ivory. Though in military bands the number of keys was confined to three, to suit march tunes, village and town bands used a variable number. Classical composers, among them Monteverdi, Schutz and Gabrielli, wrote numerous pieces for the serpent and Handel even included a serpent in his 'Music for the Royal Fireworks'. Yet despite its general acceptance the serpent aroused extreme passions in the musical world. Berlioz considered its

tone to be 'truly barbaric', while one critic pronounced the sound it made to be not unlike 'the mooing of an Essex calf'.

A typical early band would have used many sorts of instrument — serpent, bassoon, fiddle, clarinet, trombone, ophicleide, drums; and it may well have had singers as well since bands often doubled as choirs and *vice versa*. Instruments played in church bands can still sometimes be seen in honourable retirement hanging on church walls. Traditional instruments did valuable service for years until there was a revolutionary change in band music during the nineteenth century: this was the emergence of the all-brass band.

Technological developments brought about the introduction of totally new kinds of brass instruments and the adaptation of existing ones, thereby greatly improving the tone of these instruments and increasing their versatility. Fundamental to this change was the invention, in 1839, of the

21

Further refinement led to the modern cornet, one of the two great solo instruments in banding, the other being the euphonium. Bass instruments were improved by adopting compensating pistons, a device that overcame their former flatness. Other instruments such as the baritone and tuba were also introduced to extend the repertoire of bands. Indeed it gradually became possible for bands to imitate a full orchestra, albeit with varying degrees of success.

One of the most famous instrument-making firms was Distin and Company. The family originated with John Distin, an enterprising man from Devon who started his musical career playing in the South Devon Militia Band. After a seven-year apprenticeship to a Devon bandmaster he enlisted in the Grenadier Guards but later settled in London, where he played and taught the bugle. He then formed, with his sons, the Distin Quintette, which undertook tours all over Britain and abroad. In 1844, when the Quintette was performing in Paris, the Distins met Adolph Sax, the inventor of sax instruments. After this meeting the Quintette gave up their old pace-horns and adopted the famous sax-horns, a change that won universal acclaim. Eventually Henry Distin decided to give up the touring life; he settled in London and established an instrument-making firm with twenty workmen. The firm rapidly established itself and in 1867 won prize medals for its instruments at the Paris World's Exhibition.

Competition between instrument makers was fierce, with advertisements displayed in widely circulated journals like the *Orpheus* and the *Reed and Brass Journal*. Not all bandsmen welcomed the revolution, for the purchase of new brass instruments, or even second-hand ones, was expensive. Agricultural labourers and cottagers had little money to spare for new instruments so that small reed and wind bands continued until well into the nineteenth century in country areas, occasionally reinforced by a cornet or trumpet. In contrast town bands, particularly those in richer industrial areas, soon equipped themselves with brass instruments, often with the assistance of industrial benefactors.

A battered old trumpet once owned by a member of Melbourne Band, Derbyshire. As was the custom the band's name was inscribed on the bell of the instrument.

gros piston (the piston valve) by Monsieur Perinet, a Paris instrument maker. Members of the horn family, especially the cornet, became the focus of experimentation. The cornet's predecessor bore the name *cornopean;* it resulted from work done on the European continent, most importantly by the Amsterdam firm of Embach, which through a series of patents begun in 1824 evolved a complex system of tubing and valves for the new instrument. Its introduction to England was an immediate success; cornopean owners and admirers even established their own *Cornopean* magazine in order to keep subscribers informed about trade developments and general band news.

Besses o' th' Barn Band displaying a variety of cups and trophies in 1907.

THE CONTESTS

The competitive spirit amongst bands seems to have arisen first in the North of England. One of the first recorded competitions was at Burton Constable, near Hull, in 1845. Sir Clifford Constable, the local lord of the manor, arranged a band contest as a novelty attraction in the annual Burton Show, an event that included falconry, archery and sideshows. Prizes of £12 and £8 were offered to the top two bands and there was a collection for unsuccessful competitors. A platform was erected for the contest in the deer park and Richard Hall, an organist from Hull, was appointed judge. Several bands took part in the event, among them the Patrington Band, the Holmes Hull Tannery Band and the Brocklesby Yeomanry Band, and a good crowd came to observe the proceedings. A year or two later a series of regular contests was initiated at Hull by Enderby Jackson, a band conductor and sometime circus band performer. Jackson also helped organise Britain's first important band contest, which took place in Belle Vue Gardens, Manchester, in 1853.

Bands were required to have at least ten players, all of whom were to be amateur musicians. A crowd of sixteen thousand listened appreciatively as bands played items such as the 'Hallelujah Chorus' and Bishop's 'Guy Mannering' overture. After lengthy deliberations the first prize of £16 was awarded to the Mossley Temperance Saxhorn Band; second and third prizes went to bands from Dewsbury and Bramley.

In 1860 the success of contests at Belle Vue, Hull and other venues in the north was followed by a contest for bands in the south, held at the Crystal Palace, Sydenham, where six platforms were provided for the occasion. Over forty bands from throughout England and Wales entered the contest. While a panel of eighteen judges decided on the prizewinners Enderby Jackson conducted a combined band of no less than 1,390 performers in a musical entertainment for spectators. After an exhausting day prizes were finally presented in mid evening, first prize being awarded to Black Dyke Mills and second

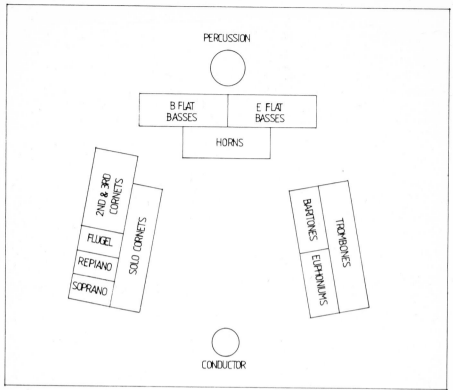

PERCUSSION

B FLAT BASSES	E FLAT BASSES

HORNS

2ND & 3RD CORNETS

FLUGEL

REPIANO

SOPRANO

SOLO CORNETS

BARITONES

TROMBONES

EUPHONIUMS

CONDUCTOR

Plan of standard band contest formation.

prize to the Saltaire Band from Bradford.

The rapid spread of contests was only made possible by an ever growing network of railways, making contests more accessible to both bandsmen and audiences. Many railway companies ran special trains on contest days and occasionally were willing to reduce fares. At one Belle Vue contest, attended by eight thousand people, railway companies laid on fifty excursion trains — and this contest, held in 1888, was fairly typical of its time. In 1885 Besses o' th' Barn Band travelled to Alloa to compete in Scotland's first ever contest, having raised the necessary expenses by playing a special football match. Lancashire and Yorkshire bands carried off all the prizes, Besses themselves winning first prize, a decision that provoked rapturous applause from the Scottish enthusiasts, who then proceeded to run riot, trampling down plants and shrubs in their efforts to see the bandsmen and pursuing them all the way to the railway station in a state of near frenzy.

Recognising the need for a national contest, J. Henry Iles, composer and music publisher, organised an experimental contest at Crystal Palace in July 1900, to coincide with the International Music Exhibition. Forty-eight bands competed for a first prize of £75 and the National Challenge or Thousand Guinea Trophy — an honour that went to the Denton Original (Manchester) Band. Initially the Crystal Palace contest was entered by reed bands, boys' bands, concertina bands and brass bands, but it was eventually restricted to brass bands. The contest became the highlight of the banding year, setting high standards that did much to raise the status of brass bands in the following years.

ABOVE: *Nantlle Vale Band (Gwynedd), about 1902, posing in front of their bandroom; a Crystal Palace cup takes pride of place at their centre. In the background is Coedmadog slate quarry.*

RIGHT: *Typical band concert programme, beginning characteristically with a rousing Sousa tune.*

Programme.

1. March ...	"Stars and Stripes" ...	...	*Sousa*
2. Overture	"l'Italiana in Algieri" ...	...	*Rossini*
3. Valse ...	... "Amoureuse"	...	
4. Selection	" Merrie England "	...	*Ed. German*
5. Danse des Bacchantes...	...	...	*Gounod*
6. Valse ...	... "Bleue"	...	..
7. Intermezzo	"Forget-me-not"	...	*Macbeth*
8. Selection	"Reminiscenses of the Savoy"		*Moore*
9. Gavotte	... "Mediæval" ...	...	*Clendon*
10. Valse ...	"Sourire d'Avril"	...	... *Depret*
11. Danses	From "Nell Gwynne" ...		*German*
12. Lied	... "Allerseelen"	...	... *Lassen*
13. March...	"With Sword and Lance"...	...	*Starke*
14. Selection	... "Carmen"	...	.. . *Bizet*

BLACKDOWN HOUSE,
23rd July, 1903.

*Two band-
stands il-
lustrated in the
catalogue of the
Milton
Castings
foundry, about
1907. The top
model is stated
to have been
erected at
Leeds,
Darlington,
Youghal, Ilford,
Hastings, Bux-
ton and Bury;
the lower one at
Altrincham,
Helensburgh,
Clacton-on-Sea
and Leith.*

Brighton's 'birdcage' bandstand was built in 1884. Below the platform was an entire 'comfort station', where holidaymakers could retreat from the hustle and bustle of the promenade.

BANDSTANDS

The first bandstands can be traced back to the latter half of the eighteenth century when fanciful pleasure domes were erected to house orchestras, and in some cases dancers too, amidst rambling gardens set out to delight the eye and provide vistas for the visiting crowds.

One of the earliest bandstands to have been built was in London's Vauxhall Gardens, while the first built specifically for bands was in Cremorne Gardens, also in London; there bands provided a glittering spectacle in an illuminated pagoda, which offered a perfect focal point for the many entertainments. The first bandstands were greatly influenced by oriental architecture. Since Sir William Chambers, a prominent eighteenth-century architect, constructed his famous Chinese tower at Kew in 1762, the pagoda had become a traditional building in English parks and gardens. Chambers was an enthusiast for all things Chinese; Chinese buildings he thought unremarkable for magnitude or richness of materials but he admired their proportions,

simplicity and beauty. He also drew attention to the Chinese emphasis on the importance of a building's precise location and he stressed the need to site a bandstand where its features would be displayed to the best effect.

These ideas proved to be an inspiration to Victorian designers who were commissioned to create islands of nature in the midst of industry. As Victorian entrepreneurs urbanised the landscape, building terrace upon terrace, mills and factories, the lack of access to fresh air and pleasant surroundings became a serious health and social problem. The Victorian solution was to create parks and gardens. Burgesses, reformers and often developers themselves made land available, often on condition that the parks were named after them. West Bromwich opened its 56 acre (23 ha) Dartmouth Park in 1878 on the instigation of the Improvement Commissioners, the land being leased from the Earl of Dartmouth. Once parks were established the people using them soon

27

Nottingham's Arboretum bandstand, erected in 1907, following a petition to the Corporation signed by several hundred ratepayers. The rustic-style bandstand cost £320 and was opened to the strains of the City Police Band.

sought entertainment. Bands, being well suited to open-air entertainment, soon found themselves with very full programmes, and never more so than in what became known as the 'summer season'.

Larger industrial towns often provided several bandstands, especially in the Black Country, where a long tradition of iron-founding reduced the cost of fabrication. West Bromwich's first bandstand was opened in 1887 in Dartmouth Park. It housed bands on two afternoons a week and there was a 'sacred' music concert on Sundays. In 1897 a second bandstand was opened at Hill Top, by the Mayor and Samuel Downing, a local ironmaster who doubtless bore a proportion of the £160 building costs. At nearby Wednesbury,

where a park was opened to celebrate Queen Victoria's Jubilee, the bandstand figured prominently until as late as the 1953 coronation celebrations when Shirley Prize Band, Keith Hampton and his Castle Rock Orchestra and Harry Engleman and his BBC Players offered an astonishing variety of music.

In the late nineteenth century band-stands were in such great demand that ironmakers included them in their catalogues. To some extent this led to a standardisation of styles as there was in-evitably a limit to the variations possible with ready-made kits. At the same time some customers preferred to put the building of their bandstand out to com-petition. Some commissioned distinguished architects, for whom the design of a bandstand must have been something of a diversion. Captain Francis Fowkes, architect of the Albert Hall in London, is known to have designed two bandstands for erection in the Royal Horticultural Society's grounds in Kensington in the 1860s. One of them was later moved to Clapham Common, where it has been used ever since. Some customers wanted something a little eccentric and a flight of municipal fancy seems to have been favoured in many seaside towns. Southend's bandstand, for example, was a monolithic extravagance adorned with classical urns, garlands and foliage, all encased by glass screens and topped by a large globe, itself surmounted by a pointed turret.

At Bournemouth, a resort with a long musical tradition, four bandstands were built for bands and other entertainments. For promenaders using the pier Bournemouth once had a fine Chinese-style stand at its pier head. Here crowds sat on benches beneath flapping canvas awnings, as Captain Featherstone conducted Bournemouth's Municipal Band or while the Municipal Orchestra played selections from its concert repertoire. In the town's Lower Pleasure Gardens stood another stand, a rustic piece with a thatched roof. Bournemouth's two other bandstands were constructed later, on public walks: Fisherman's Walk and Pine Walk. The latter, erected in 1933, took the form of a huge wooden square measuring 22 by 25 feet (6.7 by 7.6 m), complete with four sets of sliding and folding windows.

In the heyday of the British Empire bandstands spread from one end of the world to the other; bandstands were built in Valparaiso, Nassau, Monte Carlo, Milan, Poona and Calcutta. Wherever the British went, whether for business or pleasure, bandstands were sure to follow. There was no restriction on style. Some were strictly utilitarian; others rose in cakestand layers and Japanese frills. And the popularity of band music all over the world led to a multiplication of stands in parks and gardens in countries with highly individualistic architectural traditions, a factor which further enriched the diversity of styles already introduced by British designers. Though bandstands are one of the more curious products of English architecture there can be few buildings which span so many countries and exhibit such a variety of architectural styles.

Cliftonville bandstand in Kent: a picture taken in the days of Edwardian splendour.

Band Stand Oval,   Cliftonville.

29

John Gladney, the 'father' of the brass band movement. Born in Belfast in 1839, Gladney became a member of Louis Jullien's famous orchestra when he was only ten years old; in 1861 he joined the Hallé Orchestra as a clarionet player, but an increasing interest in brass instruments led him to devote himself entirely to bands, and in his long career Gladney trained and conducted more than a hundred different bands, among them Besses and Stalybridge bands.

The Cycle Band of Singer and Company, one of the many novelty bands which thrived in the nineteenth century.

THE BRASS BAND MOVEMENT

There were an estimated forty thousand amateur bands in the British Isles in 1889; one musical instrument maker had ten thousand bands on its books. By 1900 there were well over two hundred contests running every year and a National Band Festival at Crystal Palace providing a showpiece for bands and their music. The revolution brought about by the introduction of brass instruments had resulted in a small army of bands, a phenomenon that became known as the brass band movement.

In the North of England brass band music had immediately caught on as a workmen's hobby. Indeed many bands were formed from factory employees. The Meltham Mills Band from Yorkshire was formed by Jonas Brooks and Brothers, a firm of cotton thread makers, who equipped the band with instruments, uniforms and a music room. Many brass bands naturally had working-class sympathies and supported campaigns for political reform. As early as 1819 Stalybridge Old Band was engaged to play at a reform meeting on St Peter's Field, Manchester, an occasion which won infamy as the Peterloo massacre. But brass bands played at all manner of events: gar-

den parties, flower festivals, regattas, agricultural shows and opening ceremonies. They were a popular choice for railway openings. The Yarm Town Band played at the opening of the Stockton to Darlington line in 1825, and at the Rainhill locomotive trials in 1829, held prior to the opening of the Liverpool and Manchester Railway, a brass band was reported to have played 'pleasing and favourite airs'.

Increasingly bands were in demand to perform at concerts in public parks and seaside resorts. When the Victorian working classes discovered, or rather invaded, the seaside they did not go for their health, as did fashionable society, but for entertainment; and the seaside crowds liked nothing better than to stroll along the promenade to the sound of the brass bands. A lucrative summer season at a leading resort was much prized by bands and the gay tuneful overtures by Adam, Auber and Herold proved the most popular with seaside audiences and were ideally suited to blustery promenades. The popularity of bands at seaside towns continued into the twentieth century. A band contest in Skegness in June 1937 attracted the largest crowds ever seen so early in the season. A local newspaper reported that 'Thirty-three

31

special trains and fleets of motor coaches poured into the resort from an early hour ... and after the judging thousands of people assembled in the Tower Gardens to hear the massed bands play the march "Skegness Breezes". '

A variety of publications catered for the growing number of bands, with the *Brass Band News* and *British Bandsman* leading the field. Both were founded in the 1880s and were filled with articles, advertisements, contest reports and correspondents' letters. It was through these journals that the founding fathers of the brass band movement, men such as John Gladney, Alexander Owen and Edwin Swift, became household names all over Britain. In its first editorial the *British*

Bandsman unashamedly declared that the journal's aim was to 'popularise band music' and elevate its status.

During the twentieth century bands experienced mixed fortunes. After a golden age in the 1930s there were difficult times in post-war years. Bands appeared and disappeared almost overnight. It was the era of radio and television, and bands, whether originating from village, town or factory, had to adapt yet again to new circumstances. Yet if the pace and pattern of life was changing beyond recognition there was one fact that the village bandsman of the past and the bandsman of today would both recognise — that as long as there are people who want to hear band music there will be bands to play it.

FURTHER READING
Bainbridge, Cyril. *Brass Triumphant*. Frederick Muller, 1980.
Boon, Brindley. *Play The Music Play!* Salvationist Publishing, 1966.
Russell, J. F. and Elliot, J. H. *The Brass Band Movement*. Dent, 1936.
Taylor, Arthur. *Brass Bands*. Hart-Davis MacGibbon, 1979.

Front cover of the first issue of 'The Bandsman' magazine.